The
of Scripture

by Canon Michael Lewis

*All booklets are published thanks to the
generous support of the members of the
Catholic Truth Society*

CATHOLIC TRUTH SOCIETY
PUBLISHERS TO THE HOLY SEE

Contents

Preface

In one of his homilies, St Augustine recalled how the risen Christ had walked with Cleopas and his companion on the road to Emmaus. The disciples had seen the apparent collapse of all their hopes for the salvation of Israel when Jesus had been crucified. As they walked along, Christ turned their anguish into joy by opening up the Scriptures to them, showing how the Prophets had said that the Messiah had to suffer these things in order to enter into his glory. He expounded to them in all the Scriptures the things that were about himself.

Christ then appeared to the Eleven and healed their unbelief by allowing them to touch him. But, as Augustine stresses, he did not consider it sufficient simply to allow the Apostles to touch him, for

> He wanted to appeal to the Scripture to confirm their hearts in the faith. He saw us in anticipation, who had not yet been born, who do not have the chance to touch Christ but do have the opportunity to read about him.[1]

Christ went through the whole Old Testament, spanning it all in his embrace, and showed the Eleven how his suffering had been to fulfil those Scriptures. All this was for a reason. The faith of all future generations would be built on the base of those Scriptures with which Christ wanted to confirm the faith of those who touched him. Augustine goes on to comment

> The Scriptures are in fact, in any passage you care to choose, singing of Christ, provided we have ears that are capable of picking out the tune. The Lord opened the minds of the Apostles so that they understood the Scriptures. That he will open our minds too is our prayer.[2]

The Incarnate Word in his Paschal mystery is the meaning of Scripture. Christ is the key to the whole of Scripture and each constituent part of Scripture can only be understood in terms of the content and unity of Scripture as a whole.

This message is a central theme in the writings of Pope Benedict XVI, both as Pope and as Cardinal Ratzinger. In his *Jesus of Nazareth*, Pope Benedict has given us a master class on how to read Scripture, and calls us to return to Emmaus, to a Christ-centred *lectio divina* which is both simple and profound.

Pope St Leo the Great famously called on Christians to 'realise their dignity.' In our postmodern world, where everything is seen as relative, we need to realise anew the dignity of Scripture, to see it for what it is: the Word of the living God. On our part, we must be ready to be challenged by Scripture for Scripture provides the answer to the question which can shake us out of our complacency, 'What does God ask of me?' Reading the Scriptures can never be a passive experience. God engages with us in his word.

In reading Scripture, we are not boldly going where none has gone before. God has not left us orphans: he has sent us his Holy Spirit whose life in the Church finds expression in the great gifts of Tradition and the Magisterium, the teaching authority of the Church. The Scriptures flow from within the People of God and live within that People, the Spirit-filled community of the Church, the Bride of the Incarnate Word, whose book it is.

This book seeks to encourage people who might be hesitant, not to be afraid but to drink deep of Scripture and to realise anew its dignity in the light of the *Catechism of the Catholic Church*. In the Divine Liturgy of the Byzantine Rite, the Scriptures are greeted with the exultant cry 'Wisdom!' God speaks truly of God. With our eyes fixed on Christ, let us be attentive to God's word and 'taste and see that the Lord is good.'

Scripture in the Life of Christ

The Example of Christ

Everything that Christ did in his life on earth was for our instruction and as an example for us to follow. As the *Catechism* teaches:

> In all of his life Jesus presents himself as our model. He is 'the perfect man', who invites us to become his disciples and follow him. In humbling himself, he has given us an example to imitate, through his prayer he draws us to pray, and by his poverty he calls us to accept freely the privation and persecutions that may come our way.

> Christ enables us to live in him all that he himself lived, and he lives it in us. 'By his Incarnation, he, the Son of God, has in a certain way united himself with each man.' We are called only to become one with him, for he enables us as the members of his Body to share in what he lived for us in his flesh as our model. (*CCC* 520-521)

The *Catechism* goes on to quote St John Eudes:

> We must continue to accomplish in ourselves the stages of Jesus' life and his mysteries and often to beg him to perfect and realise them in us and in his whole Church. . . For it is the plan of the Son of God to make us and the whole Church partake in his mysteries and to extend them to and continue them in us and in his whole Church. This is his plan for fulfilling his mysteries in us. (*CCC* 521)

Strangely enough, there is one mystery of Christ that is often overlooked: the mystery of Christ as the perfect reader of Scripture. We forget all too easily that the incarnate Word himself read and loved the Scriptures as he received them as a child, from within the faith community of the Jewish people. The way in which Christ read the Scriptures is, of course, definitive for all who would follow him.

The constant memory of Scripture

Since at least the time of Ezra, the study of the Scriptures was central to Jewish faith. Great emphasis was placed on the education of children and on memorising the sacred text by repetition. When we speak of Christ reading the Scriptures, we should not picture him sitting down to read the sacred scrolls as we sit down to read a book: few Jews could have afforded to have their own copy of the Scriptures. Christ's 'reading' was above all an interior reading of what he knew and had learned by heart. The Son of Mary treasured God's word in his Heart.

Such memorisation was not uncommon among devout Jews, just as there are devout Muslims today who know the whole of the Quran by heart. When Christ asked the scribe what he read in the Law, he was not asking him to open a book but to look into his memory. Christ would have known by heart most if not all of the Torah, and large parts of the Prophets. Christ's intimate knowledge of Scripture reflects the religious milieu in which he was immersed from childhood, a world in which the sacred text was paramount. That text was the object of an intense and ardent love. For the Son of Abraham, the Word made flesh, as for all devout Jews both then and now, there was nothing marginal or optional about the Scriptures.

As members of Christ's body, our own reading of Scripture should be an extension and continuation in our own time and space of Christ's reading of Scripture. Christ is the context in which we read the Scriptures. Our reading should be full, active and conscious: we should read as Christ read, with all of our heart, mind and soul.

Since, obviously, the Scriptures that Christ read and loved were what we now call the Old Testament, the Jewish *Tanakh*, so we too must love the Old Testament as he did. This is part of our imitation of Christ. No Christian can ignore the Old Testament if they wish to be faithful to Christ's example. Just as Christ interpreted his mission in the light of the Old Testament in which the New Testament lies hidden, so too we shall find that the Old Testament is unveiled in the New.

The Religious Education of Jesus

Another example that Christ gives us is that of *ahavat Torah* – his love for Torah, a fervent and vibrant engagement with God's living word. Driven by the desire to study the sacred text, the Jews were the most literate of all the peoples of the Roman Empire. Both Josephus, the Jewish historian, and Seneca, the Roman writer, remark on the extraordinarily high level of Jewish religious education. By the time of the destruction of the Temple in A.D. 70, the Jews had established a nationwide system of primary schools to enable Jewish boys to study the Torah, the first organised system of primary school education in recorded history. It was in this intensely Torah-loving world that Christ grew in wisdom and in favour with God and man.

St Matthew tells us that Joseph was a zaddik, a righteous man, a pious observer of the Law. Jewish parents saw the duty of teaching children the 'words of God' as strictly commanded them by God in the Shema, the 'Hear, O Israel,' a prayer as fundamental to Judaism as the 'Our Father' is to Christianity. God's word was to be diligently taught to the young.

The Infancy narratives depict Joseph and Mary living 'according to the Law.' If we put the names of the members of the Holy Family back into their original form, we can see the Jewish context of Christ as the 'reader' of Scripture more clearly. From the beginning, Yosef and Miryam dedicated themselves to teaching the Torah to the child Yeshua. By the age of twelve, Yeshua was so advanced in his study of the Torah that he amazed the teachers in the Temple with his knowledge of the Torah in the typically rabbinic manner of answering question with question.

What the child Jesus learnt was not a set of rules and legal prescriptions but rather God's teaching and instruction, God's way for his people given out of infinite love for them and in which they delighted: in the words of the Psalmist: 'O how I love thy law! It is my meditation all the day.' Our English word 'law' does not express adequately the full meaning of the Hebrew word 'Torah' which may be better expressed as 'teaching' or 'instruction.' 'Torah' comes from the

Hebrew *root yarah*, to 'shoot an arrow' or to 'hit the mark.' The underlying theme is that Torah is God's way for man, the way to be on target, God's guide or map for his people. When Christ said that he was the way, he was essentially saying that he is our living Torah.

Written and oral

Contrary to what is often said, Judaism is not a religion of the book. The Torah has two dimensions: written and oral. In one sense, 'Torah' refers to the five books attributed to Moses, the Pentateuch, but it also refers to all the guidance and teaching given to Israel by God's revelation. 'Torah' is transmitted both in written form and in the oral tradition which both expounded and interpreted the written text. In fact, we could say that Judaism became a religion of biblical exegesis or interpretation rather than simply 'of the book.'

A Catholic will readily see how this idea of Torah corresponds very closely to Catholic teaching on the transmission of God's revelation both in Scripture and in Tradition. Along with his words, God gives a way of interpreting those words which is conveyed by tradition. For a Jew, the Bible was always the Bible as interpreted by Jewish tradition. The legal codes in the Torah state the law, but tradition was necessary in order to apply that law to the concrete case and to establish general principles.

From the beginning, there was a symbiotic union between text and interpretation, both of which were transmitted by tradition. In fact, even the reading of the text itself depended upon tradition. The Hebrew language contains no true vowels and is consonantal: it is the living memory of the community which permits the Hebrew text to be vocalised faithfully. Tradition is thus a total 'handing over' of what God has revealed to his People.

The Pharisees

In the debates that raged between the competing schools of religious thought in his time, it is significant that Christ generally sided with the Pharisees. The Pharisees supported oral tradition against the Sadducees who rejected the whole idea of oral tradition. Certainly, Christ was highly critical of the burdensome multiplication of purely human rules, especially of the elevation of minor ritual matters over the major ethical demands of justice and charity. He criticised the motives and hypocrisy of some scribes and Pharisees; but this is not a criticism of oral tradition as such, rather of its abuse. He juxtaposed the inauthentic interpretation of the Torah with his own authentic interpretation, which draws very often on the writings of the Prophets.

In Matthew 23:2-3, Christ tells the crowds and his disciples:

> The scribes and the Pharisees sit on Moses' seat; so practice and observe whatever they tell you, but not what they do; for they preach, but do not practice.

The 'chair of Moses' appears nowhere in Scripture but, by speaking of it, Christ clearly acknowledges the importance and authority of oral tradition and its interpretation. Similarly, at the Last Supper, Christ respects that oral tradition: for the grace after the meal, the reciting of a blessing over the wine in Matthew's Gospel and the singing of the Hallel Psalm after the meal, which we read about in Mark, appear nowhere in the written Torah.

As the new Moses, Christ comes to give a new Torah that both fulfils and perfects the old. Just as Christ chose to be baptised by John the Baptist because it was 'fitting,' so too with his attitude to tradition: by his own example, Christ taught that Scripture does not exist in a vacuum. There is no foundation at all in the Gospels for the Protestant view of *sola scriptura*, that the Bible alone is sufficient and that Tradition can therefore be dismissed.

Throughout the Gospels, Christ uses the characteristic phrases 'Have you not read?' and 'As it is written.' His public ministry begins with his reading from the prophet Isaiah, that is from the *Haftorah*, the selection from the prophets which followed the reading of the set Torah portion in the synagogue for Sabbath. On the cross, Christ quotes from Psalm 22: 'My God, my God, why have you forsaken me?" Christ the reader of Scripture saw his whole life as the fulfilling of those Scriptures that he had known intimately since childhood. His inner reading of the Hebrew Scriptures was a fundamental element in his own understanding of his mission.

In our prayerful reading of Scripture, we seek to be united to Christ in the mystery of his own love and meditation on Scripture, of those holy words stored in his human mind and treasured in his Sacred Heart. Christ's 'reading' and his prayer were one.

Where do the Scriptures come From?

The Sacred Text

When Polonius asked him what he was reading, Hamlet famously gave the dismissive reply: 'Words, words, words.' Whether spoken or written, words are the units of language that convey meaning and make present the thought of the speaker or writer. At the most fundamental level, Scripture is 'words,' but what words they are! In the Incarnation, the Son of God took human language in all its weakness and limitations to himself: God became man in order that he might speak to us as he had spoken to Moses, face to face, as a man speaks to his friend.

Quoting from the Second Vatican Council's *Dei Verbum*, the *Catechism* says this on the 'words' of Scripture:

> In order to reveal himself to men, in the condescension of his goodness God speaks to them in human words: 'Indeed the words of God, expressed in the words of men, are in every way like

human language, just as the Word of the eternal Father, when he took on himself the flesh of human weakness, became like men.' (*CCC* 101)

'Sacred Scripture is the speech of God as it is put down in writing under the breath of the Holy Spirit.' (*CCC* 81)

That same Spirit who hovered over the face of the primeval deep in Genesis hovered over the sea of human words, over the chaos of letters, and through the free collaboration of human writers, transmuted those words into the very words of God. Similarly, the creation of man is mirrored in the creation of Scripture. As God shaped the dust and breathed into it and it became a living man, so the Holy Spirit breathed into human words and they became words of life.

Just as the Word took our humanity to himself from the womb of the Virgin, so God takes our words in all their fragility and weakness to himself, and makes them his own. From the time of the Fathers, a parallel has been seen between the mystery of God taking human words to himself in Scripture through the work of the Holy Spirit and his taking our human nature to himself in the womb of the Blessed Virgin Mary by the work of the same Spirit.

Historically, in the temporal order, it took over a millennium for the Scriptures to come into being and to reach their final form, these marvellous words inspired by the Spirit and yet also truly authored by man. But, as the speech of God, the Scriptures were God's delight from all eternity. In all his words, the Father speaks but one Word and, in that Word, his Son, he is well pleased. Hence, in the liturgy, we declare after the reading of the words of Scripture 'The word of the Lord' rather than 'the words of the Lord,' thus emphasising the unity of Scripture. *Lex orandi, lex credendi*: the law of prayer is the law of belief.

The Enlightenment Attack on Scripture

With the eighteenth century Enlightenment, a new school of biblical criticism emerged which the Fathers of the Church would have totally abhorred. Beginning with writers such as Reimarus, a Deist, these critics dismissed out of hand even the possibility of divine intervention in human history. Their central thesis was that the 'Christ of faith' of the Church was a fabrication of the early Church. Accordingly, the object of scholarship was to seek out the 'real' Jesus of history. The result of this allegedly dispassionate quest for the historical Jesus was almost invariably a mirror image of the scholar himself.

David Strauss's *Life of Jesus Critically Examined* (1835) purported to demonstrate that Christianity was a myth. Strauss was an important influence on the young Karl Marx and was described by Nietzsche as 'incomparable.' Ernest Renan's *Life of Jesus* (1864) essentially expressed and developed Strauss's ideas in elegant French. Although now little read, both books have had a major impact on subsequent Western religious thought.

In effect, the Rationalist attack was a revival of the Gnosticism that had threatened the early Church, in the sense of a revival not of dualism, but of the intellectual pride and spiritual elitism that lay behind that heresy. Those who were 'in the know' knew that the central tenets of traditional Christianity were merely myths. The 'real' Jesus worked no miracles, did not rise from the tomb and most certainly was not the Son of God. Faith was an opiate for the weak and credulous.

Such views helped spark a crisis in the history of Christianity, especially within the Protestant tradition, that in many ways continues to this day. We have only to look at the popularity of books such as *The Da Vinci Code, The Gospel According to Judas* and the numerous sensational 'debunking' accounts of the Virgin Birth or Resurrection that proliferate in the media. Undoubtedly, such attacks on orthodoxy have provided ammunition for those hostile to Christianity, and have helped create a lingering suspicion (in the minds of those with little knowledge of Scripture) that Scripture has in some way been undermined.

In a justly famous essay called 'Fern seeds and Elephants,' C.S. Lewis wrote a devastating critique on this whole trend in Biblical criticism by homing in on its unspoken assumptions. It is an essay that should be required reading for all biblical scholars. What Lewis did was to point out the one very shaky and unconscious assumption upon which the whole case of writers such as Bultmann rested:

> All theology of the liberal type involves at some point - and often involves throughout - the claim that the real behaviour and purpose and teaching of Christ came very rapidly to be misunderstood and misrepresented by his followers, and has been recovered or exhumed only by modern scholars. ... The idea that any man or writer should be opaque to those who lived in the same culture, spoke the same language, shared the same habitual imagery and unconscious assumptions, and yet be transparent to those who have none of these advantages, is in my opinion preposterous. There is an a priori improbability in it which almost no argument and no evidence could counterbalance.[3]

Far from being objective, the sceptical school of criticism swung like a weathervane driven by the wind of the prevailing philosophical fashions of the day, whether it be Deism, Hegelianism, Marxism, liberal Protestantism or the existentialism of Heidegger.

Essentially these critics saw their role as that of distilling away in the alembic of rationalism all that was supernatural, in order to arrive at a 'pure' Christianity unpolluted by the Church. The Scriptures were seen as little more than an accidental historical accumulation of disparate historical texts with a solely human authorship and of varying subjective value.

Inevitably, the liberal critics ended up with something that was a pure construct of their own imaginings, and the confirmation of their own prejudices. In the words of F.F. Bruce, their biographies of the 'real' Jesus 'often tell us more about their authors than they do about their subject.' The sceptics were expert at looking at the tiny fern seeds, but ignored the elephant in the room, namely, the extraordinary and compelling figure of Christ.

The Way the Church reads Scripture

The Catholic Church welcomes and embraces genuine and objective Biblical criticism as a vital tool in illuminating our understanding of the sacred text, but for a Catholic the constant is always that the Scriptures are the inspired word of God, God's holy gift for his holy people. Indeed, one thing is utterly clear from even the most cursory reading of the Gospels. From the beginning, the historical Jesus evoked in those who met him a response of either faith or of rejection. His followers followed him because they had faith in him. No one could be neutral about Christ. Jesus was crucified not for preaching a simple gospel of universal love but because he claimed to be the Son of God. The Christ of faith and the Jesus of history are one.

The Church reads Scripture as a lover reads a love letter, delighting in every phrase and nuance, looking for the inner meaning, returning to it again and again, always seeking the face of the beloved and ever discovering new significance under the guidance of the Holy Spirit. The Church knows no other way of reading God's word. In this, the Church is simply being faithful to Christ's own word and example, and that of the first Christians who read the Scriptures as words possessing a divine authority.

How to Choose
a Bible

Translations

The gift of the Holy Spirit at Pentecost enabled men and women to hear the good news in their own language. Indeed, except for a handful of Aramaic phrases, Christ's words have come down to us in Greek translation. Unlike Islam, the Church has always allowed translations of the sacred text. In the West, the Latin translation of the Vulgate enjoys pre-eminence. The Orthodox Church regards the Septuagint - the Greek translation of the Old Testament – as the canonical text.

Modern translations are made from the original languages: even the classic Douay-Rheims version was translated from the Latin in the light of the Hebrew, Greek and Aramaic originals. The textual scholars who painstakingly seek to establish the most accurate text possible are the unsung heroes of biblical scholarship, and follow in a great tradition that goes back to Origen and Jerome. They work to ensure that what we receive is the pure wheat of God's word.

The 'words of the Lord' are not given to us that we might substitute our own words in their place, out of some misguided attempt to improve them. That would be ultimately for us to attempt to place ourselves over God's word and to claim to know better than God himself how he should speak to us. It is the word that forms the Church, not the other way round: the Church recognises that word and interprets it, but it is always God's word, not ours. Just as the Church cannot change the matter of the Eucharist – bread and wine – into rice and sake, so she cannot change the words of Scripture.

Dynamic and Formal

For most of us, our encounter with God's word will be by means of a translation. It follows therefore that if we wish to explore the depth of Scripture, we must exercise great care in choosing a translation of the Bible so that what we can be assured that what we read is an accurate and faithful version of the original. The question immediately arises 'Which translation should I use?' To answer that question, we need first to look at the underlying principles or philosophy of the translator.

Broadly speaking, there are two approaches to translating, both of which have their fervent supporters and opponents. The first of these approaches is known as *dynamic equivalence.*' It seeks to convey the meaning of the original text with the emphasis placed on translating entire thoughts rather than on an exact word by word translation. To achieve a translation that reads as modern, easy to understand English, idioms, style, structure, syntax, grammar and words may well be changed considerably to promote readability and ease of understanding.

The second approach is known as *'formal equivalence'* and is the opposite of *'dynamic equivalence.'* Formal equivalence aims at achieving the maximum fidelity to the text consistent with intelligibility. This approach is 'essentially literal' as it seeks to capture the precise wording of the original and the personal style of each writer. In practice, of course, no translation falls completely into one category or the other: a totally literal translation would be unreadable, and a totally free translation would be little more than a paraphrase.

Anyone wishing to go deeper into Scripture would be ill-advised to opt for a translation that is primarily dynamically equivalent, for the simple reason that it is the words that convey meaning. As every lawyer knows, change the words and you change the meaning. To take an example from the Nicene Creed, 'seen' and 'unseen' is not the same as *visibilium et invisibilium.* If I hide behind the door, I may not be seen, but I have not become invisible like the angels. Paradoxically, language that might be regarded as slightly old-fashioned is often more effective in accurately conveying meaning than more contemporary language which often proves ephemeral or carries the wrong connotations.

Biblical Hebrew is short on vocabulary but it is a wonderfully powerful and concrete language. In any good translation, something of the 'feel' of the original should remain, with something too of the personal style of the writer. A disembodied 'meaning' or 'thought' is not enough. Readability is a virtue but if what we are reading is not what is actually there in the inspired Scripture, then readability has achieved nothing and has become counter-productive. It is far better to have an explanatory footnote, or a glossary for Biblical terms that may require explanation for the modern reader, than to translate in a way that superficially appears to make the text more accessible but only at the cost of misleading the reader.

In the Prologue to Ecclesiasticus, the translator points to the difficulties of his vocation:

> You are urged therefore to read with good will and attention, and to be indulgent in cases where, despite our diligent labour in translating, we may seem to have rendered some phrases imperfectly. For what was originally expressed in Hebrew does not have exactly the same sense when translated into another language. Not only this work, but even

the law itself, the prophecies, and the rest of the books differ not a little as originally expressed.

Inevitably, all translation involves compromise and some impoverishment of the source text: the primary aim of the translator must always be to achieve the maximum fidelity to the text compatible with intelligibility within the target language.

The Vatican Instruction *Liturgiam Authenticam* reminded translators:

> The words of the Sacred Scriptures ..... are not intended primarily to be a sort of mirror of the interior dispositions of the faithful; rather, they express truths that transcend the limits of time and space. Indeed, by means of these words God speaks continually with the Spouse of his beloved Son, the Holy Spirit leads the Christian faithful into all truth and causes the word of Christ to dwell abundantly within them, and the Church perpetuates and transmits all that she herself is and all that she believes, even as she offers the prayers of all the faithful to God, through Christ and in the power of the Holy Spirit. (19)

By translating words as consistently and faithfully as possible, it becomes easier to make use of a concordance, that indispensable tool in exploring the riches of a particular word or theme in Scripture. Consistency in translating enables the reader to see the unity and coherence of Scripture and how the two Testaments complement each other.

Every Catholic home should have at least one translation of the whole Bible, not a version that excludes as 'apocryphal' those books such as Tobit and Ecclesiasticus which the Church teaches are inspired and canonical. The best policy is to have more than one translation and, where possible, an edition that has marginal cross-references which enable the reader to see how the two Testaments are inextricably linked.

Among the more formal translations, the *Catholic Revised Standard Version* is superb. It is the main version used in the English edition of the *Catechism*. Another useful translation is the *CTS New Catholic Bible*, based on the 1965 Jerusalem Bible with the Grail Psalter. In accordance with the wish of Pope Benedict, this translation uses 'Lord' for the divine Name and, although leaning more to the dynamic equivalence approach than does the *Revised Standard Version*, it does so in a balanced way.

The Word and the words

In Scripture, human language reaches its perfection. The sounds we make and the words we write are raised up to become the vehicle of revelation by God himself, who transfigures the broken speech of man. Blake said that eternity is in love with the works of time. What the Scriptures reveal is a God who is in love with our frail and imperfect human language.

The Biblical love and reverence for the human word contrasts strongly with postmodern philosophy's contention that words have no fixed meaning. The French philosopher Derrida argued that beyond the text there is nothing and that the text itself is something to be 'deconstructed' with no one authentic meaning. Christianity rejects such reductionist and sterile views. For the Christian, beyond the text there lies the God who reveals himself to his creatures; through the 'words' flows the Word himself.

The words of Scripture can only be understood within the context of a loving dialogue with the Word in the Holy Spirit. The *Catechism* puts it beautifully:

Through all the words of Sacred Scripture, God speaks only one single Word, his one Utterance in whom he expresses himself completely: you recall that one and the same Word of God extends throughout Scripture, that it is one and the same Utterance that resounds in the mouths of all the sacred writers, since he who was in the beginning God with God has no need of separate syllables; for he is not subject to time. (*CCC* 645)

It is important to remember that the Hebrew word for 'word,' *dabar*, also means 'thing.' The word is alive and active: it is a word that invites and attracts. The Son of God has the words of eternal life and man does not live on bread alone, but 'on every word that comes from the mouth of God.'

As Christians, we need to recover that ecstatic love of God's word that was the hallmark of the Fathers of the Church. Here, as always, the liturgy is our best guide on the attitude of love and thankfulness that we should have for the Scriptures. The Book of the Gospels is cherished and reverenced almost as if it were a living person. The *Catechism* expresses this beautifully:

> ... the Church has always venerated the Scriptures as she venerates the Lord's Body. She never ceases to present to the faithful the bread of life, taken from the one table of God's Word and Christ's Body. In Sacred Scripture, the Church constantly finds her nourishment and her strength, for she welcomes it not as a human word, 'but as what it really is, the word of God'. 'In the sacred books, the Father who is in heaven comes lovingly to meet his children, and talks with them.' (*CCC* 103-4)

The Word as Icon

The Scriptures are a verbal icon, a 'sacramental' of the presence of God. Traditionally, Eastern Christians speak of 'writing' rather than 'painting' an icon. Icons are a celebration of the Incarnation, of the fact that Christ the Word has been made flesh and has dwelt among us as one whom we can see, touch and hear. What the icons are in colours, so the Scriptures are in words: witnesses to the Incarnation, charged with God's presence.

For modern man, Scripture has lost its aura. Our view of Scripture has become too small. The Scriptures have become documents or literature, a 'religious book' rather than a vibrant and living gift from God – through which, above all when read liturgically, Christ speaks to us today as surely as he did by the shores of Galilee so long ago. All too easily we become overly familiar with sacred things. To 'put out into the deep' of Scripture, we need to rediscover a piety for the word, so that we might realise that the words of Scripture come 'trailing clouds of glory' from God who is our home.

Christ's presence in the Scriptures is not a substantial presence, as is his presence in the Eucharist. With the Blessed Sacrament, each visible particle is the Body of Christ and is of infinite value. Scripture has both a divine and human authorship: it did not fall like a meteor from heaven to the earth. As the Pontifical Biblical Commission expressed it:

> The thought and the words belong at one and the same time both to God and to human beings, in such a way that the whole Bible comes at once from God and from the inspired human author.[4]

The 'fundamentalist' view that divine inspiration is synonymous with God using the human authors as mere typewriters is erroneous. The inspired human authors had different and sometimes limited understanding: Obadiah and St John's Gospel are both inspired, but not of equal value. The one and the same Spirit worked all these things, distributing to each one individually just as he willed. If one may continue with the icon analogy, an icon is composed of many layers and colours, the gold of heaven and the brown of earth. God has used many artists each with their own finite human characteristics, levels of ability and vision, to produce the verbal icon of Scripture.

From this we can see that Christianity is no 'religion of the book,' any more than Judaism is. In Islam, the Arabic text of the Quran is seen as a manifestation on earth of the 'Mother of the Book' eternally present in heaven before Allah. But Christianity is a 'religion of the "Word" of God,' a Word which is 'not a written and mute word, but incarnate and living' (*CCC* 108, citing St Bernard).

What is revealed is not a Book but the Word himself: the Scriptures are the inspired witness to that Word. The Holy Spirit opens up to us the letter of the text that we might be centred on Christ, the Incarnate and living Word, and that we might not just to know the way, but walk the way with all of our being.

Interpreting Scripture

The Old in the New

Not only is Christ the perfect 'reader' of Scripture, he is also the key to Scripture. In the New Testament, this is readily apparent: Christ is the central figure on every page, above all in the four Gospels which are the heart of all the Scriptures. But for many Christians, the Old Testament can present difficulties, not least because in our modern world there is often an unconscious and inbuilt bias against anything described as 'old.' 'Old' carries with it connotations of redundancy and obsolescence. This can lead to what might be termed 'the hermeneutics of ageism': why do we need the old when we have the new? Such views unconsciously echo those of Marcion, the Gnostic heretic who rejected the whole of the Old Testament.

It goes without saying that the first Christians never saw the Hebrew Scriptures as the 'Old' Testament: they were simply part of the Scriptures in which they saw the face of Christ and which pointed to their fulfilment in God's final revelation in Christ. In fact, the earliest recorded use of the adjective 'old' to describe the

Hebrew Scriptures, as opposed to the distinction between old and new covenants, does not occur until Melito of Sardis round about 170.

Even the most cursory reading of the New Testament overthrows the Marcionite thesis. The four Gospels alone contain some seventy direct references to the Old Testament, either by quoting Scripture or by stating how Christ has fulfilled what is contained there. Indeed, the New Testament contains nearly three hundred direct references to the Old Testament, many of them quotations. Like love and marriage, the Old and the New Testaments go together.

Emmaus

In the Gospels, we see Christ depicted as the perfect Rabbi, the definitive interpreter of Scripture and Tradition, frequently quoting Scripture and revealing its meaning. Significantly, Mary of Magdala hails the risen Christ as *Rabboni*, which means both 'master' and 'teacher.'

In St Luke's Gospel, the risen Christ is emphatic on the overwhelming need for his followers to believe and to understand that he is the fulfilment of the Old Testament. Christ the Rabbi sees it as imperative that the disciples should read the Old Testament correctly.

On the way to Emmaus, upbraids Cleopas and his unnamed companion:

'O foolish men, and slow of heart to believe all that the prophets have spoken! Was it not necessary that the Christ should suffer these things and enter into his glory?' And beginning with Moses and all the prophets, he interpreted to them in all the scriptures the things concerning himself. (*Luke* 24:25-27)

Christ's words are electrifying. Cleopas and his companion say to themselves: 'Did not our hearts burn within us while he talked to us on the road, while he opened to us the Scriptures?' Christ then appears to the Apostles and says to them,

'... These are my words which I spoke to you, while I was still with you, that everything written about me in the law of Moses and the prophets and the psalms must be fulfilled.' Then he opened their minds to understand the scriptures, and said to them, 'Thus it is written, that the Christ should suffer and on the third day rise from the dead, and that repentance and forgiveness of sins should be preached in his name to all nations, beginning from Jerusalem. You are witnesses of these things.' (*Luke* 24: 44-48)

When we consider how few of the risen Christ's words have been recorded, we see the extreme significance given to these words by the early Church and how vitally important they were to the proclamation of the Good News. God's promises in the Old Testament have now been fulfilled with the coming of the Messiah and his Death and Resurrection. This truth was at the heart of the *kerygma* of the early Church, its proclamation of the Good News, and the pre-eminence of the theme of word and fulfilment in the early Church goes back directly to the risen Christ himself.

On the way to Emmaus, Christ did far more than simply satisfy the intellectual curiosity of the two disciples. Recently we have seen a plethora of books on alleged Bible 'codes.' But the life-transforming and ecstatic joy experienced by the disciples on the road to Emmaus was in a different category altogether to the jubilation felt by those engaged at Bletchley on the Ultra project (when the Enigma machine broke the German codes in the Second World War).

The disciples' hearts burned within them as Christ opened the Scriptures because he was opening up to them the infinite treasures of his own Heart, the infinity and eternity of his divine mercy, as revealed in the Scriptures. From creation itself, through the covenants with Noah, Abraham, Moses, David and the promise of the new covenant, the disciples saw that love was God's meaning from the beginning, and that this love had triumphed and was with them now.

As Francis Thompson wrote in 'The Hound of Heaven,' Christ says to prodigal humanity:

Ah, fondest, blindest, weakest,
Thou dravest love from thee, who dravest me.
I am He Whom thou seekest!

In the Scriptures we see God betrothing himself to his people for ever, and we open our invitation to the marriage feast of the Lamb.

The Memory and Unity of Scripture

Faithful to the working of the Holy Spirit who lifts the veil, the Church reads the Old Testament in the light of Christ crucified and risen. We discover the profound unity of the Scriptures as a whole, while at the same the Old Testament continues to retain its own intrinsic value as Revelation – reaffirmed by our Lord himself .

The Old Testament is charged with the glory of the New. The long story of the revelation of God's redemptive will is made radiant in the light of Easter. Take, for example, the tender and moving story of Ruth with its gracious message of the universality of God's love. It continues to retain all of its inherent beauty and charm, but with an added dimension when we recall that the Gentile convert Ruth is an ancestor of Christ himself. Christ is the one who recapitulates or sums up all things, including the Old Testament, in himself.

In reply to those who would see the Old Testament as made redundant by the New, Louis Bouyer wrote:

> What should we think of a husband and wife who, after a whole life spent together, could say to one another, 'come, let us forget our common history; let us never think any more of our first meeting, of the circumstances of our falling in love, of our honeymoon, of the birth and childhood of our sons and daughters, of all our common joys and trials through the years. Let us get rid of all that dead past. It is merely a burden which prevents us from knowing and loving each other just as we are now. Let us suppress the past entirely and live only in the present, for then our love will be far clearer and deeper than it is?' Such conduct would obviously be senseless, for the mutual love of such a couple would die if their common past was forgotten and with it their knowledge of themselves and of each other. Little or nothing would remain of their present itself if their memory of the past could be blotted out. For we are not only what our history has made us; we are in some way that history itself, memory being the basis of personal conscience as well as of personal love.[5]

The Part and the Whole

The Church teaches that the books of Scripture 'firmly, faithfully and without error teach that truth which God, for the sake of our salvation, wished to see confided to the Sacred Scriptures' (*Dei Verbum*, 11). Apparently difficult passages can best be interpreted in the light of Scripture as a whole, in which we see the sacred authors 'growing in wisdom.'

Like the facets of a diamond, each part of Scripture reflects according to its capacity the light of God's Word. By analogy, we could say that the four Gospels correspond to the facet that reflects most fully perfectly the brilliance of the light. But no facet exists by itself and in isolation from the others: it is all the facets together, their setting and context, that reveal the diamond cutter's art. The Book of Nahum may be a lesser facet than Genesis, but the craftsman cut it for a reason.

The Literal Sense of Scripture

The *Catechism* teaches that the first requirement for the correct interpretation of Scripture is that the reader should be attentive to what the human authors truly wanted to affirm, that is, to the literal sense. This involves looking carefully at the texts in the light of their *sitz in leben* - their 'setting in life.' To discover the human author's intention:

... the reader must take into account the conditions of their time and culture, the literary genres in use at that time, and the modes of feeling, speaking and narrating then current. 'For the fact is that truth is differently presented and expressed in the various types of historical writing, in prophetical and poetical texts, and in other forms of literary expression.' (*CCC* 109-111)

The biblical scholar seeks to discover the literal meaning of the text by careful study of the text, taking into account matters such as the literary, linguistic and historical context. This literal sense of Scripture is the foundation for all other interpretations but, as we shall see, it does not exhaust all other meanings which may well not have been fully apparent to the human writer at the time.

Many wrong interpretations of the Bible arise from a failure to attend to what the human authors wanted to affirm, and by ignoring the form in which they expressed themselves. Biblical Hebrew itself often uses highly anthropomorphic language of God. This does not mean that God is a human being; simply that it is a characteristic of the concrete nature of the language itself that it employs figurative language to express abstract properties. (Perhaps the supreme example of a total failure to recognise this elementary fact is the bizarre teaching of the Mormons that God the Father has a physical body.) Similarly, when looking at the creation narratives, the fundamentalists often fail to accept that the human authors might be inspired to use any literary form apart from simple historical record. The true intention of the author is thus distorted.

The True Meaning of a Text

Certain Biblical critics take it for granted that the only valid meaning of a text is to be found in its most primitive form. They argue that the true meaning – often based on their own highly personal and hypothetical reconstruction of the text – has been corrupted by the Church in subsequent readings. But Scripture is not a Russian doll which we can carefully open, until we arrive finally at the innermost doll (traditionally a baby doll), declaring that we have arrived at the one true doll. The baby doll is not the whole doll: it is the canonical text – all of the dolls put together – which is the expression of the Word of God. The canonical text is no mere accident of history.

From our own everyday experience we know that the full significance of words often only becomes apparent in the light of later events and mature reflection. A deeper significance is seen that was not fully realised at the time. Lincoln's famous Gettysburg address was written in response to an unexpected request for a 'few appropriate remarks' at the opening of a new war cemetery. The address exists in five manuscript versions, but it is the last version, signed by Lincoln himself, that is seen as the definitive text. Gradually, these few remarks, dismissed incredibly by a contemporary reporter as 'dishwatery,' came to be seen by all as one of the foundational and defining texts in American history.

The original meaning of a text as intended by the human author does not exhaust the total meaning, for there can be a deeper meaning that transcends the limited understanding of the human author. Famously, Caiaphas prophesied that it was better for one man to die for the people than for the whole nation to perish (*John* 11:50). Caiaphas made this the last prophecy of the old dispensation not on his own accord but as high priest, and without any awareness of the profound truth of his words.

Reading Scripture as a Whole

Pope Benedict has repeatedly stressed that Scripture must always be read as a whole and as a unity: individual texts must be read in the context of all of Scripture. This principle of interpretation was first explicitly enunciated in the magisterial documents of the Church at the Second Vatican Council in the Constitution on Revelation, *Dei Verbum*, but, of course, it is nothing new: it is a summary of the New Testament's own way of interpreting Scripture.

The *Catechism* teaches that the reader must be attentive both to what the human authors truly wanted to affirm (which is, of course, inspired) and 'to what God wanted to reveal to us by their words.' Necessarily, this means that we must look at the whole of Scripture, for it is always the same God who reveals. God's loving plan of salvation is not a spasmodic series of unrelated words and deeds, but marked with an internal consistency and unity of purpose.

It follows then that we shall find in Scripture what Pope Benedict has called 'the intrinsic correspondences of the faith.' As we read in Ephesians 1:10,

> God has revealed to us the mystery of his will in accord with his favour that he set forth in him as a plan for the fullness of times, to sum up all things in Christ, in heaven and on earth.

Christ is the summation of the Old Testament, which points to him as its goal.

This holistic approach enables us to resolve apparent contradictions. In some of the earlier parts of the Old Testament, for example, the human authors fail to distinguish between the direct and the permissive will of God – as in the story of the imposition of the ban on the Amalekites (1 *Samuel* 15). In the context of Scripture as a unity, we know that God wills the death of no one. According to the degree of understanding available at the time, however, the human author attributed everything to the simple and undifferentiated will of God: he lacked the theological subtlety of the Evangelists. In this case, the part has to be interpreted in the context of the whole, and cannot be seen as expressing the whole of God's Word.

The Genesis account of the creation of Eve from the side of Adam should not be interpreted as a factual account of the origin of woman. In the light of the whole, its true meaning emerges as a figure or symbol pointing to the birth of the Church from the pierced side of Christ, from which flowed blood and water, the fount of the sacramental life of the Church. The Bible is to be interpreted in the light of Christ.

The Letter to the Hebrews opens with these words:

In many and various ways God spoke of old to our fathers by the prophets; but in these last days he has spoken to us by a Son, whom he appointed the heir of all things, through whom also he created the world. (1:1-2)

These 'many and various ways' culminate in the coming of the Word made flesh. Salvation history is not the story of the disclosure of a progressive series of theological propositions about God. It is the revelation of the living Word of God, the story of an unfolding relationship initiated by God and worked out in word and deed in the lives of human beings.

Every Christian should be familiar with the basic historical outline of how God has revealed himself to man in the history of the People of God, especially through the various covenants through which he has entered into relationship with man.

We shall never appreciate Christ as the new Moses if we know nothing of the first Moses, or the significance of the new law if we have no knowledge of the old. Too often people read the New Testament with little more than a hazy and dim recollection of childhood lessons or the distortions of Hollywood. Fortunately, there are many excellent books now readily available that can remedy this. Scott Hahn's *The Father Who Keeps His Promises* is an excellent example.

Reading Scripture as a whole enables us to see what has been called the divine 'condescension' by which God comes down to the level of his growing child, much as a human father does to a growing child in order to raise him up. Together, God and man have a shared history. When we have become adults, we see how God has always been consistent, even if when as children we could not comprehend the full import of the Father's words and deeds.

This way looking at the whole picture is the New Testament's own way at looking at the Scriptures. It is the antidote to the reductionist approach that looks at Scripture in a fragmentary and atomistic way, as little more than a random and arbitrary collection of ancient religious texts.

We need look no further than Christ's own words and example. As he himself said:

> You search the scriptures, because you think that in them you have eternal life; and it is they that bear witness to me. (*John* 5:39)

In the same chapter, Christ said: 'If you believed Moses, you would believe me, for he wrote of me' (*John* 5: 46). St John comments that the lack of belief amongst the people of Jerusalem, despite the many signs that Christ had worked there, was permitted by God in order that

> ... the word spoken by the prophet Isaiah might be fulfilled: 'Lord, who has believed our report, and to whom has the arm of the Lord been revealed?' Therefore they could not believe. For Isaiah again

said, 'He has blinded their eyes and hardened their heart, lest they should see with their eyes and perceive with their heart, and turn for me to heal them.' Isaiah said this because he saw his glory and spoke of him. (*John* 5:38-41)

Here, John is quoting from Isaiah 53, the great prophecy of the man of sorrows, the Suffering Servant who will redeem his people. John gives us to understand the reason why Isaiah had said these things. It was because Isaiah had seen Christ's glory in his vision of the Lord in the Temple. John is saying that Isaiah's vision of the thrice-holy God was a vision of Christ: Christ is the Lord who sits upon the throne.

Christ came not to abolish but to fulfil the Torah. We should not be surprised to discover that the Old Testament points like a compass to its completion and fruition in the Incarnate Word and his paschal mystery.

The Spiritual Sense of Scripture

With this in mind, we come to look at the *Catechism's* teaching on the spiritual sense whereby

> Thanks to the unity of God's plan, not only the text of Scripture but also the realities and events about which it speaks can be signs. (*CCC* 117)

This fuller or spiritual sense of Scripture can be subdivided into the allegorical, moral and anagogical senses. These senses are not opposed to the literal sense, but bring out its fuller meaning in the light of Christ. As we have just been seeing, the spiritual sense is not in any way an artificial imposition upon the literal sense of extra layers of interpretation, but rather a way of exploring that sense more deeply and realising the potentiality placed there by the sacred author.

Coming events cast their shadows before. Since all of Scripture points to its fulfilment in Christ, we find 'types' or 'figures' in the Old Testament: that is, people, events, places, objects and institutions that point to their fulfilment (antitypes) in the New. In the New

Testament, the meaning and implication of these types is revealed.

Various other examples come to mind. In Hebrews 7, Melchizedek, who is both priest and king, is seen as a type of Christ. Christ himself refers to Jonah as foreshadowing his Resurrection. St Paul sees the Israelites' crossing of the Red Sea as foreshadowing the sacrament of baptism. Paul writes in Romans 5:14 that Adam was a type, a figure, of him who was to come, Christ the 'second Adam.' The sacrifices of the Old Testament point to the shedding of the blood of Christ, the Paschal Lamb. Jerusalem points to the Church and to the heavenly Jerusalem. The bronze snake lifted up by Moses in the desert points to Christ lifted up on the cross. All these take on a deeper and fuller meaning in the light of Emmaus.

In his great Eucharistic discourse in John 6, Christ is clearly referring to the manna, the bread of heaven, which nourished the Israelites in the desert as he speaks of himself as the true bread from heaven. In Jewish tradition, the miraculous reappearance of the manna, believed to have been hidden by Jeremiah, was thought to be a sign of the Last Days.

Typology thus enriches our understanding of Scripture, and is endorsed by Scripture itself. Although some of the early Christian writers pushed the allegorical approach to extremes, it remains an essential way of exploring the depths of Scripture. Following the seminal work of scholars such as Henri de Lubac and Jean Daniélou in the twentieth century, we see that this approach is rightly enjoying a revival within the Church. The literal meaning and the spiritual significance cannot be separated into two hermetically sealed containers.

The Moral and Anagogical Senses

The moral sense of Scripture is perhaps the most obvious of all the spiritual senses. As St Paul wrote:

> All scripture is inspired by God and profitable for teaching, for reproof, for correction, and for training in righteousness, that the man of God may be complete, equipped for every good work. (2 *Tim* 3:16-17)

Scripture helps us to know, love and serve God in this life and to be happy with him for ever in heaven. This moral sense is always 'Christocentric:' it is about our new life in Christ.

Scripture sets before us the great cloud of witnesses to inspire us by their example, and continually urges us not to harden our hearts but to listen to God's Word. The stories of Scripture can evoke a strong response in us, like the response of David to the Prophet Nathan's story of the unjust rich man who took the poor man's precious ewe lamb (2 *Samuel* 12). In the sacred history of God's people, we see a great metaphor for the spiritual life. Above all, we have the example of Christ, in whose death and resurrection we are called to share by dying to sin and rising to the new life of grace.

The 'anagogical' sense comes from Greek word which means literally 'leading up', and it is the meaning that causes us to raise our minds and hearts to our eternal destiny. It focuses our hope on Heaven and points to the 'four last things ever to be remembered:' Death, Judgment, Hell and Heaven.

Examples of the anagogical sense would include Christ's resurrection, as pointing to our own resurrection on the last day. Christ's miracles of healing and compassion direct our hope to the forgiveness of sin, and to the day when every tear shall be wiped away. The earthly Jerusalem is a sign of the heavenly Jerusalem of Revelation 21. Events such as the entrance of the Israelites into the Promised Land look forward to the entrance of the saints into heaven.

Of the various subdivisions of the spiritual sense, the anagogical is perhaps the least precisely defined, and is very closely related to the moral sense. It reminds us of the transforming power of God's word, directing our attention to our final goal in Christ, as it speaks to us of our final destiny through sacred event, sign and word.

Reading and Interpreting in the Light of the Spirit

In 'The Everlasting Gospel,' William Blake wrote

Both read the Bible day and night,
But thou read'st black where I read white.

Blake himself was not averse to highly idiosyncratic and bizarre interpretations of Scripture, but his words ring true. From the snake-handling Pentecostal sects in remote rural areas of the United States to liberal clerics who can so easily accommodate the Gospel to the sexual hedonism of the permissive society, we see the danger of private interpretation of the Scripture.

Fortunately, as the *Catechism* shows, we have not been left to our own devices, with each person expected to come up with their own interpretation. The sacred text was not composed by individuals living in splendid isolation, but within the faith communities of Israel and the Church. As Pope Benedict said in an allocution on St Jerome:

We cannot interpret Scripture alone, because we come across too many closed doors and fall into error. The Bible was written by the People of God and for the People of God. ... Only in this communion of the People of God can we enter 'with ourselves' into the heart of the truth that God himself wishes to tell us.

Outside of Tradition, Scripture is like a fish out of water. Without Tradition and the recognition of the authenticity of that Tradition by the Magisterium, we would not even be able to discern which writings should be included in the canon of Sacred Scripture. The Bible itself contains no list of inspired books, and indeed refers to various non-canonical books such as the book of Jasher, which have been lost. What was deemed to be inspired and what was rejected was determined by the Tradition and Magisterium of the Church, not by Scripture.

As we have seen, for a Jew, the idea of a written Torah alone without an oral Torah to interpret it would have been inconceivable. The story of Philip's conversion of the Ethiopian eunuch comes to mind (*Acts* 8:26-40). Prompted by the Spirit, Philip runs up to the Ethiopian's chariot and hears him reading from the prophet Isaiah. Philip asks him if he understands what he is reading and the Ethiopian famously replies: 'How can I, unless someone guides me?' The guidance that Philip gave to the Ethiopian in authentically interpreting the Scriptures continues to be exercised in our day by the Magisterium, the living teaching office of the Church; that is, by the successor of Peter, the Bishop of Rome, and the bishops in communion with him.

As a loving mother, the Church ensures that her children are fed with pure teaching. Ultimately, all interpretation of Scripture is subject to the judgement of the Church which 'exercises the divinely conferred commission and ministry of watching over and interpreting the Word of God.'

The *Catechism* (again quoting *Dei Verbum*) states succinctly that

sacred Tradition, Sacred Scripture, and the Magisterium of the Church are so connected and associated that one of them cannot stand without the others. Working together, each in its own way, under the action of the one Holy Spirit, they all contribute effectively to the salvation of souls. (*CCC* 95)

The connotation of words changes over the years. Our English word 'Tradition' can be misleading and carry the wrong mental associations. 'Tradition' in the Church's understanding is something dynamic rather than static. It means literally the 'handing over' of all that the Church is and believes, of all that she has received from Christ, to every new generation. Tradition is the life of the Holy Spirit within the Church. To read and interpret Scripture in the light of the Spirit is to read and interpret within the Church, 'for the Church carries in her Tradition the living memorial of God's Word, and it is the Holy Spirit who gives her the spiritual interpretation of the Scripture' (*CCC* 103).

In his commentary on St Matthew's Gospel, *Fire of Mercy, Heart of the World*, Erasmo Leiva-Merikakis wrote that Christian tradition is the 'shared life and mutual knowledge coming down to us from the Father through Jesus.' Referring to St Paul's repeated use of the Greek word for tradition – *paradosis* – in 1 Corinthians, he comments:

> The Holy Eucharist, Jesus' act of handing himself over to us in accomplishment of the Father's gift of his Son, is the supreme, living and life-giving Christian 'tradition,' from which every other authentic tradition derives.[6]

We see then the totality of what is transmitted by Tradition; the handing over of Christ himself to the Church, the Gift of gifts. With the gift of Christ comes the gift of his words, the gift of Scripture, handed down to us from the Apostles and, 'at the source, from Christ Jesus and his Father in the Spirit.'

The Magisterium is at the service of the Word of God. It is entrusted with the task of giving an authentic interpretation of the Word, whether in its written form or that of Tradition. With the help of the Holy Spirit, the Magisterium listens to the Word, guards that Word and expounds it faithfully. What Peter and the other Apostles were then, the successors of Peter and the other Apostles are now.

One of the supreme ways in which that teaching authority of the Church is ordinarily exercised in interpreting Scripture is through the *liturgy*, where day by day Christ's living Word is transmitted to us.

An excellent example of this exercise of the ordinary Magisterium of the Church is to be found in the choice of Scripture readings for the Mass of Our Lady of the Assumption. The Gospel for the Assumption is that of the Visitation, because in this Gospel St Luke shows us Mary as the Ark of the Covenant. The first reading comes from the Apocalypse which speaks of the Ark of the Covenant being found in heaven and of the woman 'clothed with the sun,' who is both Mary and the Church. The Marian title of 'Ark of the Covenant' is well known to Catholics by its inclusion in the Litany of Loreto.

In the choice of readings, we see the full sense of Scripture being opened up for us. We meditate on the eloquent parallels between Old and New Testaments to be found in the Gospel:

- Mary carries within her womb the Incarnate Word. The old Ark carried the tablets of stone on which the Ten Words (as the Jews called the Decalogue) were inscribed.

- The old Ark contained some manna from the desert. Mary contains the Bread of Life.

- Elizabeth greets Mary with the words 'Why should I be honoured with a visit from the mother of my Lord?' David greets the Ark of the Covenant with the words 'How can the ark of the Lord come to be with me?'

- David dances and leaps before the presence of the Lord in the Ark. As Mary enters the house of Elizabeth, the unborn child John the Baptist leaps for joy within his mother's womb.

- The Ark stayed in the house of Obed-Edom for three months bringing him blessings. Mary blesses Elizabeth with her presence for three months.

- Gabriel tells Mary that the power of the Most High will cover her with his shadow. The cloud of the Shekinah, the divine presence, overshadowed the tent of the Ark.

- The Ark contained Aaron's rod, the dry wood that had budded and blossomed. Mary is the Virgin who brings forth a Son.

St Athanasius spoke well when he hailed the Mother of God with these words:

> O Ark of the New Covenant, clad on all sides with purity in place of gold, the one in whom is found the golden vase with true manna that is the flesh in which lies the Godhead.[7]

The Fathers of the Church

Since the beginning, the Church as Bride of the Incarnate Word has meditated, reflected and prayed the Scriptures. She has carried them in her heart, and the soul of the Church is the Holy Spirit who gives her life.

In particular, the Fathers of the Church are outstanding witnesses to the faith and exponents of this loving dialogue with God's word. As Pope Benedict has said, in the voice of the Fathers 'echoes the constant tradition of the Church.' Pope Benedict has expressed his ardent desire that the Fathers of the Church should be seen as a fixed reference point for all theologians.

The Fathers of the Church are those writers of the early Church, down to the death of St John Damascene in the year 749, whose lives were marked by personal holiness and love of sound doctrine, and whose writings have won the approval of the Church. Many, such as Irenaeus, Athanasius and Augustine, are saints. It would be difficult to overestimate the major significance of the contribution made by the Fathers to all subsequent theology. The *Catechism* teaches:

> The sayings of the holy Fathers are a witness to the life-giving presence of this Tradition, showing how its riches are poured out in the practice and life of the Church, in her belief and her prayer. (*CCC* 78)

Above all, the Fathers explored the depths of Scripture. The second reading of the Office of Readings in the Divine Office is usually taken from one of the Fathers. Praying the Office of Readings is the best of all introductions to the Fathers of the Church.

Conclusion: Take and Read; Take and Read

We began our look at Scripture with St Augustine and it is fitting that we should close with him. In his *Confessions*, Augustine told the story of his conversion. He was in a garden in great anguish of heart when he heard a child's voice saying 'Take and read; take and read.' Taking this as a command to take up and read the book he had with him, St Paul's Letter to the Romans, St Augustine opened it up and read. God spoke to him through Scripture and turned his tears into joy. May we in our turn 'take up and read' so that our hearts too may burn within us, as did those of Cleopas and his companion as Christ walked with them on the road to Emmaus.

Endnotes

[1] Augustine On the First Letter of John, 2,1 (SC75, 151ff.) quoted in Thomas Spidlik, *Drinking from the Hidden Fountain: a Patristic Breviary* (London: New City, 1992) p. 310.

[2] *Ibid*, p. 311.

[3] C.S. Lewis (ed. W. Hooper) *Christian Reflections* (Glasgow: Fount Paperbacks /Collins, 1981), p. 197.

[4] The Pontifical Biblical Commission, *The Interpretation of the Bible in the Church* (III.D.2.c).

[5] Louis Bouyer, *Rite and Man: Natural Sacredness and Christian Liturgy*, trans. M. Joseph Costelloe (Notre Dame, Indiana: University of Notre Dame Press, 1963), p. 209.

[6] Erasmo Leiva-Merikakis, *Fire of Mercy, Heart of the World: Meditations on the Gospel according to St Matthew*, Vol. 2 (San Francisco: Ignatius Press, 2003), p. 404.

[7] Athanasius, Homily of the Papyrus of Turin, 71:216.